BECOMING UNSHAKABLE

A GUIDE TO SELF-TRANSFORMATION

KARL-HEINZ SCHRADT

GALAH BOOKS

THIS BOOK ACCOMPANIES 'BECOMING UNSHAKABLE', A YOUTUBE CHANNEL.

GALAH BOOKS

galahbooks.com

Email: galahbooks@hotmail.com

Facebook: www.facebook.com/Galahbookspublisher

©2021 Karl-Heinz Schradt

ISBN 978-0-9942886-5-3

All rights reserved. No part of this publication may be reproduced, distributed, or transmitted in any form or by any means, including photocopying, recording, or other electronic or mechanical methods, without the prior written permission of the publisher, except in the case of brief quotations embodied in critical reviews and specific other non-commercial uses permitted by copyright law. For permission requests, write to the publisher.

Cover photo: Daniel J. Schwarz

CONTENTS

INTRODUCTION 1

1. MAKING A CHANGE 5
2. ADDICTIONS AND MENTAL HEALTH 10
3. COGNITION AND THE PROCESSING POWER OF YOUR MIND 16
4. PERSONALITY FACTORS 27
5. UNHELPFUL CORE BELIEFS 36
6. TRAUMA SCREENING 56
7. MEETING YOUR BASIC NEEDS 58
8. WHAT YOU HAVE LEARNT ABOUT YOURSELF 66

CONCLUSION 82

INDEX 84

INTRODUCTION

This guide is about ideas. Ideas that are going to help us. Our minds are still primitive in some ways, always scanning the world for threats. We used to look for tigers, but now we have modern threats – financial ruin, poverty, responsibilities, complex social relationships. As modern humans, we have more control than ever over the world because we can fight disease, build cities and create computers. But we need to get better at managing our most powerful asset – our mind. Just as we shape paper into origami, we can shape our minds with ideas. In fact, the right ideas can help us tackle the issues of our inner world and help us overcome our sufferings.

How does one navigate through life without being overwhelmed? When we are young, we are filled with hope, idealism and joyful anticipation because life is full of potential and opportunities. In the same way, parents are enthusiastic when they find out that they are having a child. New life can feel like a new beginning, perhaps even a better experience than their own. But for those of us who have moved through their twenties and beyond, life isn't exactly what we thought it would be. Instead, it can feel more complicated than ever.

As a newborn, right until adulthood, you learn from those around you. You discover that life is about achievement, making others happy, behaving appropriately, keeping up appearances, having material things, money, work and status. The list of messages is almost endless. Maybe somebody told you that the secret to a good life is to become famous, accrue as much money as you can, be in a position of power or be liked.

Unfortunately, these beliefs do not align with the fundamental truth that things change. Nobody has ever lived without getting sick, aging or dying. Your bank balance, status, appearance or people's opinions cannot prevent these things from happening. Rocks, cars or opinions are created, exist for a time and then get destroyed or cease to exist. Stars burn out. Money can be valuable today but worthless tomorrow. In short, there are no certainties in life.

So what do we do? Well, we can't give up on everything. To some extent, having a satisfying job, money and a good reputation are positive things, but we can't let those things define us. If something is not completely in your control (which includes most things), you should not count on it or build your sense of self on it, nor should you sacrifice your personal and mental health in exchange. Our fortunes are subject to change and our luck is not in our hands.

In a nutshell, we start from a place of mistaken core beliefs and a lack of awareness that we are short on time. As a result, we find that we are fighting against a force that scientists call entropy. We are becoming older, sicker and closer to our demise. So, we need to ask ourselves some important questions. What quality of life do we want while we are alive? Do we want to be unhappy or angry? Do we want to suffer and spend our time experiencing addiction, having bad relationships and feeling miserable?

If you don't want to suffer unduly, your aim should not be fame, money or approval. Instead, you should be content with whatever comes your way. You have a degree of control in your life, but how life's events unfold are not always in your control. You can kick and scream and act like a victim, but life will not become fairer. You cannot assume that someone is keeping score or that your suffering will end. Instead, be grateful for where you are and how far you have come, and acknowledge that things could potentially be worse.

Our goal is to become experts at defending ourselves from suffering. We want to be the most adaptable, flexible and wise version of ourselves. We want the ability to differentiate between what is worthwhile and what isn't. Ultimately, this is achieved by addressing our thoughts and emotions. We need to identify unhelpful thoughts in ourselves and use these to recognise our triggers. By cultivating new ways of processing these feelings and thoughts, our emotions will eventually stabilise.

In this guide, I'm going to give you the tools and strategies that can help you get your life back on track. Whether you are struggling with self-confidence, lack of direction or emotional instability, I will give you a system that can help you reach your goals. What's more, you can readily tailor it to your situation and needs.

I'll begin by explaining why you may be struggling and how you can work towards a place of favourable stability. Like self-assembly furniture, there is a lot to unpack, and as we progress, you'll see how the parts interconnect. The techniques I use in this book are drawn from stoicism, phenomenology, existentialism, Buddhism and a variety of concepts from psychology, such as cognitive behavioural therapy (CBT) and motivational interviewing (MI).

This is the first of two books. In **Becoming Unshakable: A Guide to Self-Transformation**, we identify problematic core beliefs that shape our thinking and how they get us into trouble. We also examine how our brains cope with day-to-day problems and come up with pragmatic solutions. The second book, **Rewrite Your Narrative: An 8-Step Action Plan to Change Your Life**, will build on these ideas and show you how to fulfil your potential and find your true self. But before you scale that mountain, you need to do some endurance training first. So let's get started.

1. MAKING CHANGE HAPPEN

How do you know it's time to change? It could be a nagging sense that you aren't where you should be, could be or want to be. Maybe you're sick of feeling the way you do and have a wall up to the world. You may have seen someone die or had a close call yourself and the illusion of your existence has been shattered. Perhaps wine doesn't look like your best friend anymore or you've suddenly realised that your partner doesn't love you. You are scared, but you have a sense that something else exists. It's like a coffee that wakes you up and creates a new motivation, a new direction.

Imagine if you could lift the veil and peek at a new set of possibilities. What would you do if you left the fear, doubt and limitations behind you? This guide will help you do that, but it will also make you as resilient as possible when you find yourself in one of these unhelpful states.

Over the next few chapters, you will be guided through a process of introspection and self-development. You will notice traps before you get caught in them – and recognise them as unhelpful. If you are in one of these traps now, recognition of your predicament is the first step. The next step is to get out and make sure you never fall into that trap again. But that isn't enough. You need to be able to climb a mountain as well. Once you've climbed that mountain, you'll be able to look out over the landscape and see clear paths through the bushes, forests or rocky terrain that may or may not be out there.

CHECKLIST

Below are some common indicators that you are caught in habitual patterns or making choices that are limiting your potential. Answer 'Yes' or 'No' to the following.

1. I believe that my situation and mood is the fault of another person, agency or circumstances outside my control.

2. I am always depressed, anxious and burnt out.

3. I have signs of a chronic stress response, such as inflammatory conditions, headaches, migraines, digestive problems and muscle tension, but with no clear cause despite rigorous medical testing.

4. I feel like a 'threatened species' that lives in fear and lacks self-confidence.

5. I see myself as a fool who keeps making the same mistakes.

6. I lack direction and cannot act.

7. I'm addicted to a substance, drug, food, person, behaviour or relationship.

8. I experience anxiety, hatred, anger, guilt, fear, envy, defensiveness or other stressful emotions regularly.

9. I cause problems for others or myself for amusement, or because of my impulsive behaviours and thoughts.

10. I think I deserve money, attention or gifts because I am important or somehow better or smarter than others.

Answering 'Yes' to any of the statements above suggests that you have an issue that is adversely affecting your quality of life.

In this guide, my goal is to take you from a position of vulnerability or despair and make you into a hero or heroine who can overcome suffering – someone who can develop skills to succeed regardless of life's challenges.

The next part of the exercise is designed to understand yourself. You need to do some self-observation and introspection. However, this process is quick and painless. The first thing you need to do is ask yourself the following question: Is there a problem with my life as it is now?

THE FOUR LS

You are going to use several tools to understand your predicament. The first is called the 'Four Ls'. This tool is drawn from MI therapy. The Four Ls represent four different ways that problems in our lives can manifest. They stand for Livelihood, Love, Liver and Law.

The first L is for Livelihood, which refers to our work and general functionality. Are you able to function reasonably in your life? Are you able to work? Are you able to do meaningful things, keep your house clean, keep your life ordered, maintain your car, turn up to work on time and concentrate? Or are you often missing work, arriving late, unable to function, getting fired or living in a state of chaos? If you answered 'Yes' to any of these questions, then that would be a good indicator that there is a problem. Jot down some thoughts you have about this.

The next L is for Love, which refers to relationships. Reflect on the relationships you have, maybe with a significant other, your family, friends, colleagues or with the world at large. Are your relationships functional, satisfying and reciprocal? Take a moment now to reflect on this and make a note of what you would like to improve.

The next L is for Liver, which refers to our health, either physical or mental. In terms of mental health, this could be depression, anxiety, addiction or a lack of self-worth. If we are not looking after ourselves physically, this could mean eating junk food or drinking excess alcohol. We could have a health problem we are not addressing, like a fatty liver, or maybe our concentration is suffering because we smoke marijuana or use some other drug. Reflect now and try to be thorough. Think of health risks you take, such as having unprotected sex, base jumping, boxing or fighting. What activities may lead to suffering, either through injury or severe disability?

The final L is for Law. Do you tend to get into trouble with the police or fined for breaking the rules? Do you get scolded by bosses and get complaints from neighbours? Or do you have a lengthy criminal record? These are signs of being in a rut. Reflect now and determine what thoughts and behaviours got you into trouble, and what could have been avoided.

2. ADDICTIONS AND MENTAL HEALTH

We are complex beings with motivations, drives and social needs. Our nervous systems, hormones and neurotransmitters can slow us down, relax us or speed us up thanks to millions of years of evolution, dietary changes, ways of thinking and activities. Over time, however, humans have found foods, drinks and substances that can shortcut the way they feel. Sadly, our delicate systems are easily broken and imbalanced, and we can lose ourselves in these dependencies and addictions.

Take a moment to reflect on whether you may have an addiction that you could start to address. I also encourage you to self-screen for mental disorders as it may help you determine if those issues are present.

ALCOHOL AND SUBSTANCE USE

Let's rate your alcohol and substance use and see if this could be a reason why you can't move forward. Alcohol and substance problems often create secondary anxiety and depression issues. Take some time now to answer the questions below.

Alcohol – Basic Screen

1. Do you have a drink containing alcohol more than once a week?

2. Do you have more than two drinks containing alcohol on a typical day of drinking?

3. Do you ever have six or more standard drinks on one occasion?

4. Do you sometimes find that you cannot stop drinking once you start?

5. Did you fail to go to work or tend to relationships and responsibilities because of drinking in the last six months?

6. Do you need a drink first thing in the morning to get yourself going?

7. Do you sometimes have feelings of guilt or remorse after drinking?

8. In the last year, have you ever been unable to remember what happened after a bout of drinking?

9. Have you injured yourself or someone because of your drinking?

10. Has a relative, friend or healthcare worker been concerned about your drinking in the last year?

If you answer 'Yes' more than three or four times, you may have a drinking habit. It is recommended that you seek advice on this issue.

Substance Use – Basic Screen

1. Do you use drugs other than alcohol more than once a month?

2. Do you use more than one type of drug on the same occasion?

3. How many times a day do you use drugs?

4. Are you heavily influenced by drugs more than once every six months?

5. Did you fail to go to work or tend to relationships and responsibilities because of drugs?

6. Over the past year, was your craving for drugs so intense that you could not resist it?

7. Do you sometimes have feelings of guilt or remorse after using drugs?

8. Do you sometimes find that you cannot stop using drugs once you start?

9. In the last year, have you ever been unable to remember what happened after using drugs?

10. Have you injured yourself or someone, physically or mentally, because of your drug use?

11. Has a relative, friend or healthcare worker been concerned about your drug use in the last year?

12. Do you need drugs in the morning to start the day?

If you answer 'Yes' more than three or four times, you may have a drug habit. It is recommended that you seek advice on this issue.

Note: For both alcohol and substance use screening tools, the more times you say 'Yes', the more serious the issue is. Addictions are problematic and can lead to harm or death. Seek professional advice on both activities.

MENTAL ILLNESS

The next exercise is to screen for signs of severe mental disorders. If you have any doubt, contact a psychologist, psychiatrist or mental health team in your area. Again, this is just a process of understanding yourself better and being able to notice when you need to adjust. It also helps to make a note of any patterns that come up, such as a tendency towards anger or anxiety.

The following exercise may point you towards a problem that you haven't dealt with yet, whether it be an addiction, a history of trauma, an inherited illness or a tendency towards negative thinking. For some mental illnesses, the best intervention may be medication or professional talking therapy.

Mental Illness – Basic Screen

Have a look at the questions below and answer honestly.

1. Do you have feelings of anxiety, suicidality, hopelessness, low self-esteem or irritability?

2. Do you have dramatic mood swings?

3. Do you have feelings of excessive fear, worry or anxiety?

4. Does your social withdrawal interfere with your work, interpersonal skills or physical functioning?

5. Have there been dramatic changes in your eating and sleeping habits or a decline in your care?

6. Have you dropped out of school, work or social activities? For example, have you quit sports, failed exams or found it difficult to perform familiar tasks?

7. Do you have problems with thinking, concentration, memory, logical thought and speech?

8. Do you have increased sensitivity to sights, sounds, smells or touch?

9. Do you have a vague feeling of being disconnected from yourself or your surroundings? Do you experience a sense of unreality, even if passing or brief?

10. Do you think you are 'special', being watched or chosen in some way?

11. Do you have feelings of paranoia?

12. Have others noticed that your behaviour is unusual? For instance, could they tell that you 'zoned out', were talking to yourself or doing something out of character, like yelling at the moon?

13. Do you ever think of harming yourself, other people or property?

14. Are you prone to risky behaviour, such as unprotected sex, gambling, driving erratically, fights or dangerous hobbies?

15. Do you see, feel, hear, taste or smell things that other people cannot?

Answering 'Yes' to any of the above questions warrants a visit to your general practitioner. If you or your GP are concerned about your health, see a mental health team or a psychiatrist.

3. COGNITION AND THE PROCESSING POWER OF YOUR MIND

We cannot escape our mind. It works hard to interpret what happens to us. There is a lot of incoming information that we need to interpret and compare to what came before. We need to access memories, read faces, anticipate the future. Unfortunately, if we max ourselves out, we don't function as well, which means that we make more mistakes and react rather than respond.

With this in mind, the next questions are about your ability to pay attention and think clearly. There are a couple of tools that we are going to use for this, but you can also look to your own experiences. Do you often find yourself getting distracted? Is it hard to pay attention while working or doing tasks? Often, the reason why a person feels overwhelmed is that they have too many things going through their mind. This can be due to past trauma, too much stress or unhelpful core beliefs, such as wanting fame, approval from others or perfection. Thoughts, feelings, traumatic memories or demands on yourself tend to trigger a fight or flight response, which takes up a lot of your brain's focus. If you find yourself thinking and worrying constantly, that is an issue we can address. For now, I'd like to take an objective measurement of your focus, attention and intellectual quotient (IQ).

We're not focusing on IQ because we want to improve it or make you feel smarter than others. We'll be looking at it in relation to our processing power. If you have a smartphone or laptop, you'll be well aware of the high processing speed of your device. This processing speed allows for faster functionality of applications, which means that more tasks can be done at the same time. When I talk about IQ, I'm referring to your processing power. This will help you understand whether you can load yourself up with thoughts and tasks or whether you should reduce these to function more efficiently. To find out your IQ, go to the internet and type 'simple free IQ test'. Find one that suits you and complete it.

While doing the IQ test, you might notice that you are required to hold several bits of information in your head while solving a problem. This could be sequences, shapes, colours or numbers. You are then required to scan numerous possibilities for answers to problems. This situation is like life and work. You have tasks, obligations and responsibilities you need to manage. You can't do or resolve them all at once, so you hold them in your cognitive processes. In an IQ test, you need to identify patterns, then check and validate your guesses. When you reach the end of your cognitive capacity, your attention can wane and you want the task to be over and done with. As a result, you may pick any answer or make an educated guess.

If you thought you had a very high IQ and discovered that it was fairly average, you may be overestimating your ability to process information under pressure. In this case, it would be unwise to pick a profession that requires you to think quickly or complexly in a chaotic environment. You need to work within your capabilities. It would also be unwise to spend your life performing tasks that 'overclock' your brain or that you don't have the raw processing power to complete. For example, I know that I'm not smart enough to be a physicist or a professor of economics, so I wouldn't put myself in that situation. This premise is refreshing to many because society often exclaims that 'you can do anything you put your mind to.' This is untrue and an unhelpful simplification of life's complexities.

It's important to have a job that challenges you, but you don't want to be overloaded all the time. You may have the burden of a needy partner and run a social club, which can eat into your cognitive reserves. You may try to work harder to do more but be aware that cognitive compensation takes up a lot of energy and resources.

As we move through this guide, you will see that there are ways we can reduce the load on your brain's processing ability by removing trauma and cycles of thought that are redundant or unhelpful. There are also ways to adjust your personality traits to assist your performance when you reach the limits of your IQ. In some cases, you can improve your concentration through the practice of mindfulness. There are also things that you can do to manage attention difficulties, such as simplifying your life goals or your environment. A simpler life makes it far easier to focus on important things that you need to address.

We all have a limited capacity for stress, and when we exceed that capacity, we can increase our suffering with negative emotions or thoughts and mental illness. There are two ways we can prevent exceeding our limit. The first is to reduce stressful thoughts and demands by managing our expectations. The second way is to manage our limits by using coping strategies such as talking to others, keeping pets, exercising, meditating, listening to music and so on.

NEGATIVE THINKING STYLES

The next assessment is taken from CBT. This will allow you to understand the kinds of content misrepresentations you might be experiencing on a day-to-day basis. Have a look at the list below, which is a summary of the most common negative thinking styles.

1. **Polarised thinking.** Believing that you (or certain things) are either 'the best' or 'the worst' as a result of your default yes/no thinking. This ignores all other possibilities that lie in between.

2. **Assumed pattern-finding.** You notice something once or twice and assume it is a pattern. For example, 'People never use the rubbish bins provided!'

3. **Negative biasing.** Seeing only your mistakes and faults and not your strengths/accomplishments. For example, your wife compliments your meals but tonight she doesn't say anything. As a result, you think, 'This meal is bad. I'm a bad cook.'

4. **Assuming the outcome.** You believe you can predict the future, even though the end is the result of complex factors and unpredictable events. For example, 'America and North Korea will blow up the world this year in a nuclear war. I need to build a bunker.'

5. **Assuming others' reactions.** Predicting how others will respond to things. For example, you clean the office as asked but assume your boss will be angry because you moved the bookshelf to the hallway to make space. Instead, he is thrilled and says, 'That's much better! Now we have more room!'

6. **Making a mountain out of a molehill.** You take an event or experience that may be small and make it into something huge. For example, your partner doesn't say goodbye as he leaves for work, so you assume he is planning to leave you. In reality, he was running late and didn't want to wake you.

7. **Positive blindfold.** Taking a view of life, an event or an experience that is only based only part of the evidence. For example, 'I don't think working here is worth it because of my crabby boss'. However, you ignore the fact that you love working with your clients.

8. **Puritan thinking** (e.g. should, would, must). Believing or creating rules about the world that are not universal or based on the law of your country. These 'should' and 'must' terms are instead based on your parents' opinions, cultural beliefs, the belief of a friend, church, group or person. For example, 'People should take weddings seriously and must attend if invited.'

9. **False mea culpa.** Wrongly taking responsibility or ownership for things that are not your fault or in your control. For example, 'It is my fault that the poor go hungry.'

10. **Pigeonholing.** Putting yourself, someone or something into a pigeonhole, like calling them an 'idiot' or 'loser'. This ignores the complexity of the person or thing being pigeonholed.

11. **Treating emotions as facts.** Assuming that your emotions are directly related to what is happening. For example, it is raining and you feel sad. As a result, you believe the rain is making you miserable. In reality, your thoughts are responsible for this feeling, not the rain.

CASE STUDY

Let's understand these errors by applying them to a situation. For example, your car, a Fiat Uno from the late '90s, won't start. As a result, you're going to be late for work. To make matters worse, you've been late three days in a row. As you keep turning the key, you hope that the car will start. The following thoughts may cross your mind:

1. 'This car is terrible. I don't think I've ever had such a bad car!'

2. 'Everyone at work is going to think I'm a mess and that I don't care about the morning meetings!'

3. 'I've made a mess of work this week. Three days late in a row!'

4. 'This is the last straw. My boss told me she's not happy with my work performance. She'll probably give me a written warning!'

5. 'I bet my boss will be furious!'

6. 'The company's profits were down last quarter. They'll probably fire me and the whole team, then everyone will blame me and firebomb my house!'

7. 'Life's a nightmare! There's nothing good about it!'

8. 'I should have replaced this car long ago. I must make it up to my team. Maybe I should apologise to everyone!'

9. 'It's my fault the whole company's sales are down. I didn't convince the Davis company to renew their contract!'

10. 'I'm such a loser. I can't even afford a decent car!'

11. 'I'm such a mess right now. I probably have dementia or I'm losing my mind.'

As you can see, these thoughts align precisely with each negative thinking style I outlined at the start. Take a moment now to think about what cognitive habits and thought patterns you might have. It may also be helpful to photocopy this page and reflect on the kind of thoughts you're having throughout the day. Further, if you find that you're feeling particularly anxious, angry or upset, it may be useful to stop and scan your thoughts to see if any of these cognitions are happening.

For now, it's enough to say that the painful and unpleasant emotions we experience could be indicators of automatic cognitions that are getting us into trouble. Our thoughts, especially after they become habitual, can happen so fast that we don't even notice them. Initially, it can take some practice to catch them and recognise them as 'half-formed notions'. This is because your brain has got into the habit of producing them automatically. It may be useful to talk about stressful situations with a friend or support person so that you can work together to reflect on the situation and identify the thoughts you're having.

But it isn't enough to identify these thoughts. We need to question their validity and make them more realistic. In other words, we need to make them less about personal opinion and more about the objective truth of the situation.

One way of thinking about this process is to treat your negative cognitions like a prosecution lawyer in a courtroom. The prosecution seeks to attribute blame to find someone guilty. When you reorientate your negative cognitions, you are taking the role of the defence attorney instead. You create an argument that defends you against the prosecution's accusations and provides a narrative that is realistic rather than emotional, subjective or blaming. To show you how this works, I will take the example of the car and turn each negative cognition into a realistic thought.

1. **Negative cognition:** 'This car is terrible. I don't think I've ever had such a bad car!'

   Realistic cognition: 'This car isn't terrible. I've had it for four years and haven't had a problem until today. It's one of the most reliable cars I've ever had. So, it's not fair to say that it's bad. It's quite a good car for $800. It's cheap to run and I like it!'

2. **Negative cognition:** 'Everyone at work is going to think I'm a mess and that I don't care about the morning meetings!'

   Realistic cognition: 'People know that I value meetings, so I shouldn't make assumptions.'

3. **Negative cognition:** 'I've made a mess of work this week. Three days late in a row!'

   Realistic cognition: 'Well, I have been late most of this week, but I'm generally very reliable and not often late. Anyway, I always make up for it at the end of the day.'

4. **Negative cognition:** 'This is the last straw. My boss told me she's not happy with my work performance. She'll probably give me a written warning!'

   Realistic cognition: 'My boss pointed out some areas for improvement, but then she told me I'm doing better than most. Ever since the market slowed down, it's been hard making as many sales as I would like. It's not my fault that the market's bad, and I think my boss understands that. Why would they fire an employee who's doing better than others?'

5. **Negative cognition:** 'I bet my boss will be furious!'

    Realistic cognition: 'Well, I guess I don't know if she'll be furious. She might understand because she knows that I have an old car and often talks about how she used to have a similar car. She may understand that both old and new cars have problems from time to time.'

6. **Negative cognition:** 'The company's profits were down last quarter. They'll probably fire me and the whole team, and then everyone will blame me and firebomb my house!'

    Realistic cognition: 'Maybe I'm being a bit dramatic. Everyone I work with is nice and we all get a bit stressed sometimes. I don't think anyone would ever firebomb my house!'

7. **Negative cognition:** 'Life's a nightmare! There's nothing good about it!'

    Realistic cognition: 'You know what? I have a lot to be grateful for. This job has worked out better than I thought. I'm so lucky to have this car too! I've managed to keep it running for years instead of getting into debt buying a new car. Now I have money for a deposit on an apartment!'

8. **Negative cognition:** 'I should have replaced this car long ago. I must make it up to my team. Maybe I should apologise to everyone.'

    Realistic cognition: 'There's no law saying that I must replace an old car, especially one that's been so reliable. Anyway, everybody's late now and then, and everybody can have a bad day or week.'

9. **Negative cognition:** 'It's my fault the whole company's sales are down. I didn't convince the Davis company to renew their contract!'

    Realistic cognition: "That's silly. One hundred and twenty people work at Wilson Wheels International. One person can't ruin a company!'

10. **Negative cognition:** 'I'm such a loser. I can't even afford a decent car!'

    Realistic cognition: 'Just because a person has an old car, doesn't make them a loser! When it comes to managing my money, I'm the opposite of a loser. I'm not paying interest on a loan for a new car I didn't need.'

11. **Negative cognition:** 'I'm such a mess right now. I probably have dementia or I'm losing my mind.'

    Realistic cognition: 'I'm just a bit stressed. I've had trouble sleeping recently and the car issue is just another stress. I'm probably a bit anxious because I've been busy and overtired. It doesn't mean that there's anything wrong with me or my health. Everybody has problems.'

When you confidently identify negative cognitions and change them into realistic cognitions, you will start to feel better. You will recover from problems and slowly change your mental habits, leading to less negative emotions like anxiety, anger, depression or frustration.

Lastly, a quick note about CBT. If you want to know more about the subject, I recommend the book *Feeling Good: The New Mood Therapy* by David D. Burns. It goes into detail about negative thoughts and the therapy itself. CBT is a proven method that can help you think like a stoic, improve your resilience and cut through the challenges of life.

4. PERSONALITY FACTORS

Now I would like to take a moment to talk about the OCEAN test. This test is based on findings by scientists and psychologists who undertook extensive research on human personality types. It was noted that people, regardless of culture, race and context, share many common traits. These were categorised into five personality types that remain remarkably consistent. The OCEAN model reveals areas of strength and weakness that can move you forward or hold you back. Below is an elementary OCEAN test for you to complete.

Elementary OCEAN Test: The O-10

1. I see myself as extroverted, enthusiastic.
   - ☐ Completely agree   (+4 points)
   - ☐ Kind of agree   (+2 points)
   - ☐ Neutral   (0 points)
   - ☐ Kind of disagree   (-2 points)
   - ☐ Completely disagree   (-4 points)

2. I see myself as critical, quarrelsome.
   - ☐ Completely agree   (-4 points)
   - ☐ Kind of agree   (-2 points)
   - ☐ Neutral   (0 points)
   - ☐ Kind of disagree   (+2 points)
   - ☐ Completely disagree   (+4 points)

3. I see myself as dependable, self-disciplined.
   - ☐ Completely agree   (+4 points)
   - ☐ Kind of agree   (+2 points)
   - ☐ Neutral   (0 points)
   - ☐ Kind of disagree   (-2 points)
   - ☐ Completely disagree   (-4 points)

4. I see myself as anxious, easily upset.
   - ☐ Completely agree   (+4 points)
   - ☐ Kind of agree   (+2 points)
   - ☐ Neutral   (0 points)
   - ☐ Kind of disagree   (-2 points)
   - ☐ Completely disagree   (-4 points)

5. I see myself as open to new experiences.
   - ☐ Completely agree   (+4 points)
   - ☐ Kind of agree   (+2 points)
   - ☐ Neutral   (0 points)
   - ☐ Kind of disagree   (-2 points)
   - ☐ Completely disagree   (-4 points)

6. I see myself as reserved, quiet.
   - ☐ Completely agree   (-4 points)
   - ☐ Kind of agree   (-2 points)
   - ☐ Neutral   (0 points)
   - ☐ Kind of disagree   (+2 points)
   - ☐ Completely disagree   (+4 points)

7. I see myself as sympathetic, warm.
   - ☐ Completely agree   (+4 points)
   - ☐ Kind of agree   (+2 points)
   - ☐ Neutral   (0 points)
   - ☐ Kind of disagree   (-2 points)
   - ☐ Completely disagree   (-4 points)

8. I see myself as disorganised, careless.
    - ☐ Completely agree   (-4 points)
    - ☐ Kind of agree   (-2 points)
    - ☐ Neutral   (0 points)
    - ☐ Kind of disagree   (+2 points)
    - ☐ Completely disagree   (+4 points)

9. I see myself as calm, emotionally stable.
    - ☐ Completely agree   (-4 points)
    - ☐ Kind of agree   (-2 points)
    - ☐ Neutral   (0 points)
    - ☐ Kind of disagree   (+2 points)
    - ☐ Completely disagree   (+4 points)

10. I see myself as conventional, uncreative.
    - ☐ Completely agree   (-4 points)
    - ☐ Kind of agree   (-2 points)
    - ☐ Neutral   (0 points)
    - ☐ Kind of disagree   (+2 points)
    - ☐ Completely disagree   (+4 points)

For each question, score as follows:

Openness/Concreteness .... Add Q5 + Q10 = Total

Conscientiousness/Non-conscientiousness .... Add Q3 + Q8 = Total

Extroversion/Introversion .... Add Q1 + Q6 = Total

Agreeableness/Disagreeableness .... Add Q2 + Q7 = Total

Neuroticism/Emotional Stability .... Add Q4 + Q9 = Total

Place your results on the graph below.

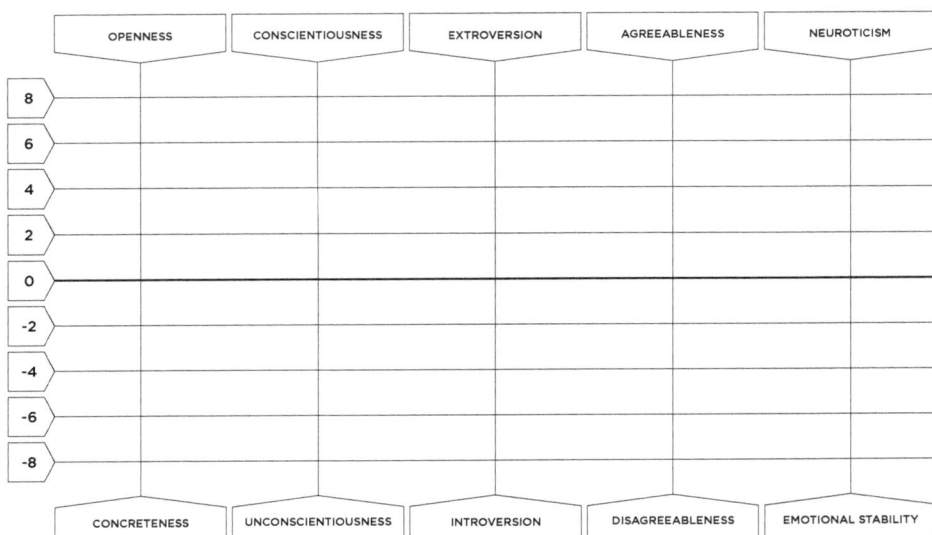

Openness

In the acronym OCEAN, O stands for openness, which refers to a willingness to expose ourselves to new experiences and ideas. For example, I might be learning about a modern philosophy or a new theory in science, and I might be open to learning more about it before I dismiss it. Motivation to keep learning is a sign that I have a high degree of openness.

Is openness desirable or harmful? Well, it's a little bit of both. If I'm too open, I might entertain ideas that are harmful to me. For example, I might believe that essential oils can cure cancer, or I might eat foods with unknown ingredients. Being too open can expose us to risks that may have detrimental effects on our lives.

However, if I'm far too concrete (i.e. lacking in openness), I am not willing to give new ideas a chance. For example, I might think that a scientific explanation for everything is the only way. You are concrete when you base your opinions and reasoning purely on what is in front of you. People who are concrete may also lack imagination as they are set on specific outcomes. If you tend to base your worldview on scientific facts, you become stale. The world is incredibly complex, often too complex to be measured by research. Many things lack concrete conclusions, like the nature of consciousness or the force behind the universe. By understanding how open you are, you can determine if you need to be more rational or open in life.

When it comes to openness, it is best to be somewhere in the middle. Somewhat open, but also relatively concrete with an ability to be flexible. If you're inventing something, it's important to be more open. When you're visiting a warzone, careful planning may be worthwhile.

Conscientiousness

The next trait is conscientiousness, which is your ability to dedicate yourself, work hard and perform well. For instance, a conscientious person is unlikely to sweep dirt under a mat. A non-conscientious person won't bother to sweep the floor at all! In life, it's vital to be somewhat conscientious. You are more likely to be productive, reliable and rewarded with financial stability and opportunities if you save money, pay off debt and don't waste your earnings.

However, you don't want to be too conscientious and let other people use your energy for their gain or be so busy that you can't slow down and relax. On the other hand, if you're not conscientious, you won't be able to deal with different problems that life throws your way. You won't be able to hold down a job and earn money to meet your basic needs, which are essential for your mental and physical health. That's why it's important to work on this trait. Nonetheless, it might be quite affirming to realise that you're more conscientious than you thought.

Extroversion

The next trait is extroversion, with introversion as its opposite. As you may know, extroversion means that you prefer other people's company, spending time at parties or environments with lots of other people, interacting, talking, cooperating or having a very social time. On the other side is introversion, where people like to spend a lot of time alone. Perhaps they want quiet time so that they can be alone with their thoughts and focus on their goals.

Once again, both sides have their pros and cons. Interestingly, being too extroverted can sometimes indicate emotional instability. This is because people may feel anxious or alone in their own company. For that reason, extroversion could be a sign of deep-rooted issues, such as unresolved trauma. Not all extroverts are traumatised, of course. Achieving focus is more straightforward when you're alone and undistracted. That's why introspection is a handy and therapeutic skill to have.

In general, human beings need to cooperate and work together. You'll achieve more with others than you will by yourself. Being alone with your thoughts for too long, with no feedback and input from others, can work against you. As a result, find a balance between extroversion and introversion.

If you tend towards one extreme, it is reasonably easy to compensate for this. For example, if you're always introverted, it may be useful to spend time with others. On the other hand, if you find that being by yourself is overwhelming, experiment with being in your own company, maybe when cooking or mediating.

Agreeableness

The next trait is agreeableness, with its opposite being disagreeableness. Agreeable people are easy to get on with and can often achieve a lot more in team environments that require cooperation. However, if you are too cooperative, you can be perceived as too wishy-washy or easily pushed around by other people. That's why an excessive amount of agreeableness becomes a problem. Being too disagreeable, however, is also a problem. Being grumpy, set in your ways or unlikable will mean that people will not want to cooperate with you or help you. This can limit your opportunities and ability to have satisfying relationships.

If you're overly agreeable, try to be more assertive and disagree from time to time. If you are excessively disagreeable, you might benefit from some CBT. Look at the content of your thoughts that are fuelling your disagreeableness and cultivate more openness. Either way, if you find yourself on the extreme end of the scale, try to move more towards the centre.

Neuroticism

The final trait is neuroticism. This trait sits on the opposite end of emotional stability. A neurotic person tends to worry, ruminate and doubt themselves.

If you spend a lot of time worrying, doubting yourself and ruminating over things that have happened, you may be too neurotic. Neuroticism takes up a lot of energy, leads to sleepless nights and increases cortisol and adrenaline, which can affect your physical and mental health. Being too neurotic is not at all helpful. You can treat neuroticism, to some degree, with CBT, which we've already discussed. Mindfulness and meditation are also beneficial.

On the opposite side of neuroticism is emotional stability. On the outside, it would appear to be a beautiful notion. However, it is also possible to be too emotionally stable. For example, psychopaths are people who commit hideous crimes with no sense of guilt and remorse. They are too emotionally stable. They can do something very impulsive and horrible without guilt, anxiety, fear or self-criticism. Psychopathy is an example of how emotional stability gets in the way of cooperating with others and living a good and healthy life. As a result, we should aim to be somewhat emotionally stable and not too neurotic.

The Middle Way

As we've gone through OCEAN, you might have noticed that a general theme has emerged about taking a middle road between extremes. This is an idea from Buddhism. Some describe the Buddha's teachings or dharma as 'The Middle Way', which is a good mantra for living a fulfilled life.

The Buddha is one of the world's great philosophical thinkers. It is generally believed that he was born into nobility, great wealth and limitless access to sports, food, drink and sexual pleasures. However, he quickly found that this life gave him little happiness. So he fled his home and adopted a completely different lifestyle. He starved himself, avoided pleasures and lived under a tree. But he found this unsatisfying too. After much reflection, he discovered that the greatest satisfaction came from living in balance and harmony, being moral and kind, and avoiding puritanism of any kind. This was a great revelation to him and became known as his 'enlightenment'.

There is a lot we can learn from Buddha's life and philosophy. Extremes of any kind are unhelpful and damaging – even when they're positive. This is why the 'Middle Way' is so important. It's not always easy, but it can help us achieve a more balanced approach to life, other people and ourselves.

5. UNHELPFUL CORE BELIEFS

There are core beliefs or ways of looking at the world that are shared by people prone to nervous breakdowns, depression and anxiety. These beliefs are stories we tell ourselves that have been internalised from outside sources. Advertisers and people who seek to influence or emotionally control us often encourage us to believe these narratives. Because we take these narratives to heart and they become our way of interacting with the world, we become defensive when they are questioned.

But these narratives breed negative emotions and are like a drop of ink in a cup of water. They taint the whole solution and make you see life as depressing, hard and unfair. Worse still, they disempower you and turn you into a victim. In the next exercise, we will screen for these beliefs with the Unhelpful Core Belief Tool.

Answer the questions on the following pages. Don't try to overthink them. Go with your gut instinct. An honest assessment will improve your self-knowledge.

Unhelpful Core Belief Tool – Section A

1. A criticised person would naturally be angered or distressed by the criticism.
   - ☐ Completely agree   (0 points)
   - ☐ Kind of agree   (1 point)
   - ☐ Neutral   (2 points)
   - ☐ Kind of disagree   (3 points)
   - ☐ Completely disagree   (4 points)

2. Pleasing other people is more important than pleasing myself.
   - ☐ Completely agree   (0 points)
   - ☐ Kind of agree   (1 point)
   - ☐ Neutral   (2 points)
   - ☐ Kind of disagree   (3 points)
   - ☐ Completely disagree   (4 points)

3. If people don't approve of you, you'll be unhappy.
   - ☐ Completely agree   (0 points)
   - ☐ Kind of agree   (1 point)
   - ☐ Neutral   (2 points)
   - ☐ Kind of disagree   (3 points)
   - ☐ Completely disagree   (4 points)

4. If people you care about expect something from you, then you should give it to them or do what they expect.
   - ☐ Completely agree   (0 points)
   - ☐ Kind of agree   (1 point)
   - ☐ Neutral   (2 points)
   - ☐ Kind of disagree   (3 points)
   - ☐ Completely disagree   (4 points)

5. If others think you have little value, then it's probably true.
    - ☐ Completely agree   (0 points)
    - ☐ Kind of agree   (1 point)
    - ☐ Neutral   (2 points)
    - ☐ Kind of disagree   (3 points)
    - ☐ Completely disagree (4 points)

Subtotal A = _____

Unhelpful Core Belief Tool – Section B

1. You can't be happy unless someone loves you.
    - ☐ Completely agree   (0 points)
    - ☐ Kind of agree   (1 point)
    - ☐ Neutral   (2 points)
    - ☐ Kind of disagree   (3 points)
    - ☐ Completely disagree (4 points)

2. You can't be happy if others dislike you.
    - ☐ Completely agree   (0 points)
    - ☐ Kind of agree   (1 point)
    - ☐ Neutral   (2 points)
    - ☐ Kind of disagree   (3 points)
    - ☐ Completely disagree (4 points)

3. If others do not include or accept you, it's because you're not normal in some way.
    - ☐ Completely agree   (0 points)
    - ☐ Kind of agree   (1 point)
    - ☐ Neutral   (2 points)
    - ☐ Kind of disagree   (3 points)
    - ☐ Completely disagree (4 points)

4. If you cannot find love, then you are probably unlikable.
    - ☐ Completely agree   (0 points)
    - ☐ Kind of agree   (1 point)
    - ☐ Neutral   (2 points)
    - ☐ Kind of disagree   (3 points)
    - ☐ Completely disagree   (4 points)

5. You cannot be content if you're alone.
    - ☐ Completely agree   (0 points)
    - ☐ Kind of agree   (1 point)
    - ☐ Neutral   (2 points)
    - ☐ Kind of disagree   (3 points)
    - ☐ Completely disagree   (4 points)

Subtotal B = _____

Unhelpful Core Belief Tool – Section C

1. All normal and acceptable people have talent or appeal.
    - ☐ Completely agree   (0 points)
    - ☐ Kind of agree   (1 point)
    - ☐ Neutral   (2 points)
    - ☐ Kind of disagree   (3 points)
    - ☐ Completely disagree   (4 points)

2. Life is purposeless and meaningless if you are not creating something of value.
    - ☐ Completely agree   (0 points)
    - ☐ Kind of agree   (1 point)
    - ☐ Neutral   (2 points)
    - ☐ Kind of disagree   (3 points)
    - ☐ Completely disagree   (4 points)

3. Useful people have ideas; useless people do not.
    - ☐ Completely agree   (0 points)
    - ☐ Kind of agree   (1 point)
    - ☐ Neutral   (2 points)
    - ☐ Kind of disagree   (3 points)
    - ☐ Completely disagree   (4 points)

4. Useful people do well and achieve; useless people don't achieve anything.
    - ☐ Completely agree   (0 points)
    - ☐ Kind of agree   (1 point)
    - ☐ Neutral   (2 points)
    - ☐ Kind of disagree   (3 points)
    - ☐ Completely disagree   (4 points)

5. You are useless if you can't do your job well
    - ☐ Completely agree   (0 points)
    - ☐ Kind of agree   (1 point)
    - ☐ Neutral   (2 points)
    - ☐ Kind of disagree   (3 points)
    - ☐ Completely disagree   (4 points)

Subtotal C = _____

Unhelpful Core Belief Tool – Section D

1. If you can't do something well, don't do it at all.
    - ☐ Completely agree   (0 points)
    - ☐ Kind of agree   (1 point)
    - ☐ Neutral   (2 points)
    - ☐ Kind of disagree   (3 points)
    - ☐ Completely disagree   (4 points)

2. You need to appear strong. Showing weakness would be embarrassing.
   - ☐ Completely agree   (0 points)
   - ☐ Kind of agree   (1 point)
   - ☐ Neutral   (2 points)
   - ☐ Kind of disagree   (3 points)
   - ☐ Completely disagree   (4 points)

3. Always be number one at whatever you do.
   - ☐ Completely agree   (0 points)
   - ☐ Kind of agree   (1 point)
   - ☐ Neutral   (2 points)
   - ☐ Kind of disagree   (3 points)
   - ☐ Completely disagree   (4 points)

4. Never make mistakes. It is normal to feel bad if you do.
   - ☐ Completely agree   (0 points)
   - ☐ Kind of agree   (1 point)
   - ☐ Neutral   (2 points)
   - ☐ Kind of disagree   (3 points)
   - ☐ Completely disagree   (4 points)

5. If you don't aim for the top, you'll end up being average and unremarkable.
   - ☐ Completely agree   (0 points)
   - ☐ Kind of agree   (1 point)
   - ☐ Neutral   (2 points)
   - ☐ Kind of disagree   (3 points)
   - ☐ Completely disagree   (4 points)

Subtotal D = _____

Unhelpful Core Belief Tool – Section E

1. You should get what you want, especially if you are certain that you deserve it.
   - ☐ Completely agree   (0 points)
   - ☐ Kind of agree   (1 point)
   - ☐ Neutral   (2 points)
   - ☐ Kind of disagree   (3 points)
   - ☐ Completely disagree   (4 points)

2. When things or people stand in the way of what you want, it is normal to feel angry or outraged.
   - ☐ Completely agree   (0 points)
   - ☐ Kind of agree   (1 point)
   - ☐ Neutral   (2 points)
   - ☐ Kind of disagree   (3 points)
   - ☐ Completely disagree   (4 points)

3. If you prioritise other people's desires, they owe you when you need it.
   - ☐ Completely agree   (0 points)
   - ☐ Kind of agree   (1 point)
   - ☐ Neutral   (2 points)
   - ☐ Kind of disagree   (3 points)
   - ☐ Completely disagree   (4 points)

4. If you're good to people, you will be loved and adored.
   - ☐ Completely agree   (0 points)
   - ☐ Kind of agree   (1 point)
   - ☐ Neutral   (2 points)
   - ☐ Kind of disagree   (3 points)
   - ☐ Completely disagree   (4 points)

5. If you treat people well, they will treat you well in return.
   - ☐ Completely agree   (0 points)
   - ☐ Kind of agree   (1 point)
   - ☐ Neutral   (2 points)
   - ☐ Kind of disagree   (3 points)
   - ☐ Completely disagree   (4 points)

Subtotal E = _____

Unhelpful Core Belief Tool – Section F

1. If you have a close relationship with someone, you are responsible for their emotions and behaviours.
   - ☐ Completely agree   (0 points)
   - ☐ Kind of agree   (1 point)
   - ☐ Neutral   (2 points)
   - ☐ Kind of disagree   (3 points)
   - ☐ Completely disagree   (4 points)

2. If you give someone advice and they get upset, then it's your fault.
   - ☐ Completely agree   (0 points)
   - ☐ Kind of agree   (1 point)
   - ☐ Neutral   (2 points)
   - ☐ Kind of disagree   (3 points)
   - ☐ Completely disagree   (4 points)

3. Whenever you see a person in need, you are obligated to help them.
   - ☐ Completely agree   (0 points)
   - ☐ Kind of agree   (1 point)
   - ☐ Neutral   (2 points)
   - ☐ Kind of disagree   (3 points)
   - ☐ Completely disagree   (4 points)

4. Parents are responsible if their children become emotional or badly behaved teenagers.
   - ☐ Completely agree   (0 points)
   - ☐ Kind of agree   (1 point)
   - ☐ Neutral   (2 points)
   - ☐ Kind of disagree   (3 points)
   - ☐ Completely disagree   (4 points)

5. The best people can please everyone.
   - ☐ Completely agree   (0 points)
   - ☐ Kind of agree   (1 point)
   - ☐ Neutral   (2 points)
   - ☐ Kind of disagree   (3 points)
   - ☐ Completely disagree   (4 points)

Subtotal F = _____

Unhelpful Core Belief Tool – Section G

1. When bad things happen, bad feelings follow and they cannot be controlled.
   - ☐ Completely agree   (0 points)
   - ☐ Kind of agree   (1 point)
   - ☐ Neutral   (2 points)
   - ☐ Kind of disagree   (3 points)
   - ☐ Completely disagree   (4 points)

2. Emotions are not in your control and you can expect to feel bad in life.
   - ☐ Completely agree   (0 points)
   - ☐ Kind of agree   (1 point)
   - ☐ Neutral   (2 points)
   - ☐ Kind of disagree   (3 points)
   - ☐ Completely disagree   (4 points)

3. Moods are the result of things that people cannot control, such as their status, wealth, genes, gender, hormones and 'internal clock'.
   - ☐ Completely agree   (0 points)
   - ☐ Kind of agree   (1 point)
   - ☐ Neutral   (2 points)
   - ☐ Kind of disagree   (3 points)
   - ☐ Completely disagree   (4 points)

4. If bad things happen in your life, you will feel bad.
   - ☐ Completely agree   (0 points)
   - ☐ Kind of agree   (1 point)
   - ☐ Neutral   (2 points)
   - ☐ Kind of disagree   (3 points)
   - ☐ Completely disagree   (4 points)

5. If good things happen to you, like good looks, status, fame or winning the lottery, then you will be happier than other people.
   - ☐ Completely agree   (0 points)
   - ☐ Kind of agree   (1 point)
   - ☐ Neutral   (2 points)
   - ☐ Kind of disagree   (3 points)
   - ☐ Completely disagree   (4 points)

Subtotal G = _____

Scoring

Add the five points in each subtotal together and write the total in the subtotal space in each section. For example:

Section A
Q1. Neutral – 2 points
Q2. Neutral – 2 points
Q3. Completely agree – 0 points
Q4. Kind of disagree – 3 points
Q5. Completely disagree – Points

Therefore, 2 + 2 + 0 + 3 + 4 = 11.

Do this for Subtotals A, B, C, D, E, F and G.

Section A Subtotal = _____

Section B Subtotal = _____

Section C Subtotal = _____

Section D Subtotal = _____

Section E Subtotal = _____

Section F Subtotal = _____

Section G Subtotal = _____

Place your results on the graph opposite.

Unhelpful core beliefs

VALIDATION	ADORATION	ATTAINMENT	FAULT-FINDING	PRIVILEGE	OBLIGATION	PASSIVITY

Here's an example of a graph that's been filled in.

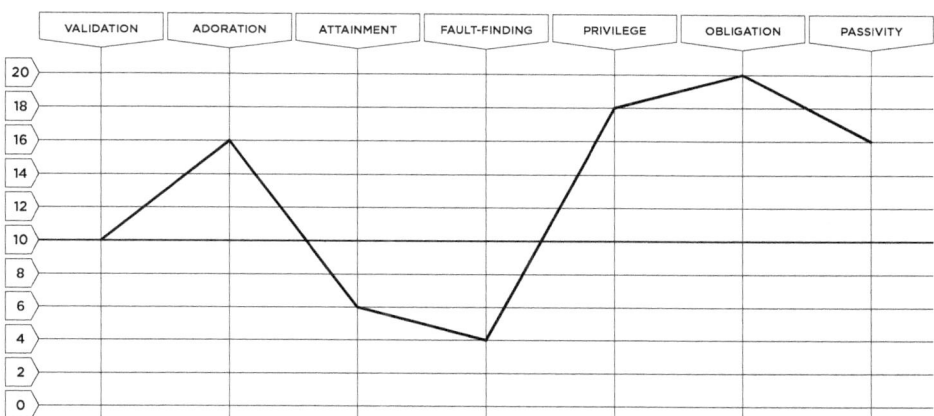

Ten is the middle of the scoring range. If your score is closer to zero, you are more vulnerable to unhelpful core beliefs. If your score is closer to twenty, you are more resistant to being dragged down by that dysfunctional world view. Looking above, we can see that this person is vulnerable to attainment and fault-finding and that they could also improve their attitude to validation. On the other hand, we can see their strengths: they do not rely on external sources of love or adoration, nor do they expect to get their way, feel responsible for things they don't control or get caught in a victim mentality.

I need to mention that being resilient to all unhelpful core beliefs isn't always positive. This is what happens with psychopaths or people with serious personality disorders. However, striving for validation, love, achievement and a sense of responsibility towards others can be a good thing, as long as we don't get too caught up in them.

Why Internal Narratives and Beliefs Matter

Healthy core beliefs allow you to control your feelings, thoughts, body, destiny and decisions. In psychology, this is called the Locus of Control. When we take ownership of our emotions and thoughts in response to the world and other people, we can manage our experience of life more effectively.

In the modern world, we have more control than ever – over disease, our lives and even nature. But by and large, we cannot control the world and other people, even though we may try. Sometimes, controlling makes things worse. In life, luck is not on our side, or we miscalculate the whole thing and it all goes wrong. But if we have wisdom and some understanding, we can manage ourselves and how we think about what happens to us.

Narratives and Core Beliefs That Make You a Victim

Let's go back to your results from the Unhelpful Core Belief Tool. If you noticed a significant vulnerability, acknowledge it and work on it. When these thoughts/beliefs come up, deal with them before they become problematic. If you don't, they will cause overthinking and worry, and you'll direct your energy towards something that doesn't benefit you. Now we'll take a closer look at what these core beliefs mean and how they can affect you.

Validation

If you think your worth is based on how people react to you and continuously seek their validation, you become vulnerable to depression, self-hatred and mental illness. Why is this? When it comes to taste and opinions, everyone is different. Because of everyone's circumstances and experiences, some people are kind, open or understanding, whereas other people are rigid and uncaring. Therefore, no matter who you are as a person, there will be people who will not like or approve of you, and it is not in your control. Therefore, it's best to identify your desire for validation, accept that you have this tendency and gently let it go.

If you are vulnerable to this need, you may seek validation by doing this in your relationships, on Instagram or even with strangers. Some amount of positive feedback is useful to know what we are doing well and what is working. But we can't let ourselves become 'validation junkies'. A balance is needed. It would help if you aimed to score at least above ten after six months of following this guide.

Adoration

If you base your worth on whether you are loved and adored, then you are vulnerable to despair. We are social animals, and we need other people and loved ones to some degree. But then again, people are fickle. People fall in and out of love and can make promises and not keep them. People change, as do their thoughts and feelings. Therefore, having a wide range of interests, support people and a strong sense of self-worth are valuable.

If someone does not love you, you cannot make them. There is no law saying they, or you, for that matter, must love anyone.

Love junkies can be a turn-off for people who value autonomy and the freedom to be themselves. Surprisingly, the less you need love, the easier it seems to find. Remember, romantic love is not the only form of love, and as people get older, they see this. Companionship is priceless, and you don't need a ring, money or looks for that kind of love. Again, a balance is necessary. You should aim to score at least below ten after six months of following this guide. The higher your score, the better, as long as you don't become selfish and callous.

Attainment

Attainment is a different type of addiction. If your score is below ten, you may be a workaholic and find it hard to relax. You may find it hard to be content unless you are always productive, active and achieving new goals. Again, balance is the key. Creativity and productivity are positive, but they are not everything. Balance these with relationships, hobbies and relaxation. When the stock market crashes, you don't want to be one of those people who are so emotionally tied to money and productivity that they fall into a deep depression or contemplate suicide. Remember, there have been countless kings, pharaohs and empires of gold and treasure throughout history. Where are these achievements now? They are buried in the sand or worn away and never to be seen again. At best, these achievements are ruins or museum exhibits, but the people themselves are gone. Live for the experience of life and not just your bank balance.

Fault-Finding

A low score in this area indicates you can't complete a task until you think it's perfect. Your idea of perfection requires stress, work and effort — so much so that your body, mental health and even your relationships suffer. When things aren't quite right, you are frustrated and bothered. You are prone to criticising yourself and others. Fault-finding is a treadmill because your work is never satisfactory. What was once perfect falls into disrepair and new tasks always keep coming. So, you can never relax and enjoy the fruits of your efforts. The truth is, the world is full of faults. Even the Mona Lisa has chips and is slowly falling apart. Eventually, you have to say that your effort is 'good enough' and move on. If your actions are reasonable, meaningful and flexible, then let that be good enough.

Privilege

When you are given things in life too easily or your parents or loved ones enable bad habits, you may start to think that you deserve those rewards. If this happens for a long time, you could develop a sense of privilege. A score below ten could suggest that you think the world owes you. You expect to get that job because you applied, and you wish to receive praise because 'this is me we're talking about'. The result? You are often annoyed or angry that you didn't get treated like royalty. A sense of privilege can ruin a life, spoil relationships and opportunities, and create negative emotion in yourself and others. Instead, learn to expect frustration, get used to disappointment and you will feel calmer and more in control.

Obligation

Have you scored below ten in this category? Maybe you tend to blame yourself when bad things happen. A friend is sad, a plane crashes or someone loses their job, and you, for some reason, have a sense of guilt or responsibility. You have a feeling that the suffering of others is your responsibility. However, because you have no control over much of the world, you have little control over the events that happen to you or others. Hence, there is no point beating yourself up about the inevitable ups and downs of life. Allow people the freedom to experience their own lives and make their own choices and mistakes. You are not their keeper – and they are likely to appreciate that.

Victimhood

A low score here suggests that you believe contentment comes from the outside rather than the inside. You sail on the sea of fate, hoping that the gods will give you fame, money and good looks, that other people will fix your problems. You may feel that you can't help your reactions to things and that there is nothing you can do to change how you cope with and see life.

On the other hand, a high score suggests that you understand that your mind creates the world, not vice versa. You understand that your interpretation and stories about the world change how you see things and feel. Hence, whatever the world and other people do, you tell yourself to adjust, rather than expecting other people to fall in line. This doesn't mean that you can't stand up for yourself, or that you accept other people's bad behaviour. No, when you have a high score, you know the difference between being a victim and setting clear boundaries about how you wish to be treated. You understand that being a victim is about sitting around blaming and complaining, and that's not you at all. You're able to stand up for yourself and take positive and assertive action.

THE JOHARI WINDOW

Another way you can improve your self-knowledge is by using the Johari Window. This tool was designed by Joseph Luft and Harry Ingham in 1955 to help people know themselves better, improve themselves, and understand how relationships with other people can help them grow. The four squares in the table below represent the information and insights that exist about you in the world. If you want to learn more about yourself, you need to expand into all boxes.

For example, you may have a way of talking that offends others and is often seen as brash, unfriendly and disagreeable. But due to your psychological defences or a lack of concern, you may not realise the offence you cause and the cost it has on others and yourself. However, the Johari Window can help you to see the value of being open to feedback and admitting that you don't have all the answers.

Open-Self Room What you and I both know about me (shared knowledge)	**Blind-Self Room** What you know about me that I don't know
Hidden-Self Room What I know about me that you don't know	**Unknown-Self Room** What you and I don't know about me (hidden potential)

Open-Self Room

This window represents those characteristics that are known to yourself and others. For example, you and I both know I wrote this book.

Blind-Self Room

These are blind spots that are not part of our awareness. For example, you see that I have a spider on my back, but I can't see it.

Hidden-Self Room

This window represents the things that we know about ourselves but that are unknown to others. For example, I know that I overfed the class goldfish in primary school, but no one else knows that.

Unknown-Self Room

This is our unknown potential. For example, nobody, including me, knows I will write another book that will sell out in Japan.

Learning About Yourself

If you want to know more about yourself, one of the best ways to do it is to receive feedback from others. Try to accept input and insights from family, friends and strangers without getting defensive. This feedback could make you stronger, wiser and help you achieve your goals.

Sometimes, however, friends don't always want to tell you the hard truth about yourself. They want to remain on good terms or your side. Or they may benefit from your malicious behaviour, which means they'll refuse to tell you the truth. Hopefully, you'll have someone honest and trustworthy who can give you feedback on the problem areas in your life.

Another way you can learn more about yourself is by journaling. This is an effective way to express your thoughts, beliefs and emotions by writing them down and visualising them in front of you. This enables you to identify patterns in your feelings and cognitions so you can address them.

7. TRAUMA SCREENING

Before moving forward, it is important to find out if there is trauma in your past that has not been dealt with. We will use the T-10 screening tool to assess this.

We can be traumatised for many reasons. It could be the conditions of our childhood, such as physical, sexual or psychological abuse. Perhaps we lived in terrible conditions and had no consistent parent figure. Or we had little sense of security and safety. Maybe our childhood was fine, but our first workplace was toxic and unpleasant. Perhaps we experienced discrimination, natural disasters or an abusive relationship.

Sometimes we 'bounce back' from trauma(s) with no real harm done. Sometimes we build shells around ourselves or have ways of coping that don't suit our needs anymore. We may believe things about ourselves that are not true, and which are the voice of an abuser or group that didn't value and understand us.

Trauma can be tricky to unravel. Like scars, they can be deep or shallow; they can be forgotten, hidden or gruesome reminders. They can even be valued and seen as signs of our growth and resilience. If you are aware of a great trauma in your life and you think it is still weighing on you, find someone to discuss it with. Take the time to process it, put it into context and see what you can change and cannot change. Sometimes, trauma presents as a post-traumatic stress disorder, and the tool below will screen for that. Trauma or relationship counselling can be an invaluable tool, but if you are experiencing the symptoms below, consider visiting a psychiatrist and, if you can, a psychologist as well.

T-10 Trauma Screening Tool

In the past month, how much were you bothered by the following:

1. Repeated, disturbing and unwanted memories, or dreams of a stressful event or trauma?

2. Repeated and disturbing dreams of a stressful event?

3. Suddenly feeling as if you're reliving a trauma?

4. Being triggered by something that reminds you of a stressful event?

5. Having a sense of panic and/or anxiety when remembering a traumatic event?

6. Avoiding something that reminds you of a stressful event?

7. Trouble remembering important parts of a stressful experience?

8. Having strong negative beliefs or feelings about yourself, other people or the world?

9. Feeling distant and cut off or finding it hard to experience positive feelings?

10. Trouble falling or staying asleep?

If you answer 'Yes' four or more times, it might be useful to seek therapy to reduce your stress response and prevent past trauma from affecting your day-to-day life.

8. MEETING YOUR BASIC NEEDS

In this section, I will explain a five-tier model that outlines our hierarchy of needs in life. It will help you prioritise your most basic needs to improve your mental wellbeing. We are going to start with the most fundamental things. What are the essential items we need to live?

American psychologist Abraham Maslow identified a theory that arranged human needs into a hierarchical pyramid shape, with basic needs at the bottom and more high-level needs at the top. He identified that everyone had basic needs, but only the wisest and most disciplined could accomplish the pyramid's tip. According to Maslow, a person could only move up the tier after achieving each level of needs. See the pyramid opposite.

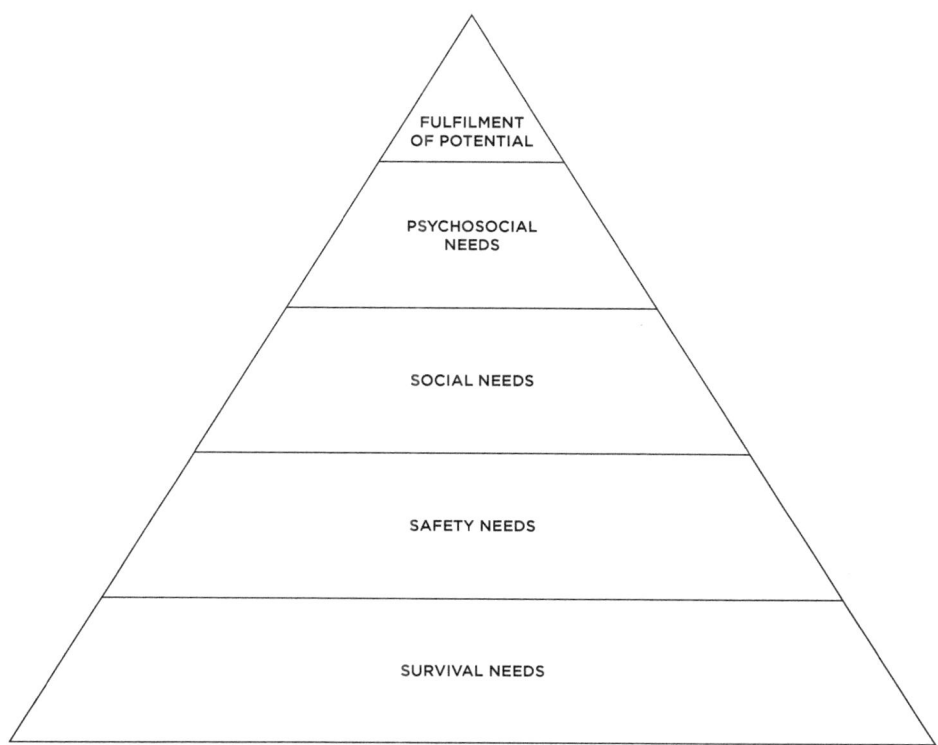

At the bottom, we begin with basic physiological needs for survival, including food, water, rest, clothing, shelter and health. The second tier outlines safety needs, such as income and protection from crime, emotional turmoil and illness. The third tier refers to social needs that influence our mental health status, such as friendships, family bonds, spouses, partners. In other words, it is our desire to be rewarded emotionally, physically or sexually. The fourth tier is about psychosocial circumstances, including self-respect, confidence, the potential for growth, acknowledgment from others and positive self-assessment. The final tier is fulfilling your potential as a person, such as becoming educated, skilled and refining your talents and strengths.

ACHIEVING YOUR FULL POTENTIAL

My goal is to help you become a resilient person who can cope with suffering, whether it comes from others, the world or yourself. To become that person, you must first meet your basic needs. See the list below.

- Ensure you have regular food, water and shelter.

- Go outside, get some exercise, organise your house, move from room to room and open the curtains.

- Get up and go to bed at the same time every day.

- Avoid undersleeping or oversleeping.

- Switch your smartphone to blue light mode and do not fight your night-time tiredness by watching 'just one more video/episode/film'.

- If an application upsets or triggers you, delete it for good. Set your phone to 'No notifications'.

- Act on what you care about. Don't complain or get upset. Take positive action.

- Set yourself specific, measurable, achievable, realistic and time-specific goals (also known as SMART goals).

- Point your internal compass towards improving your life.

- Make sure you have an essential degree of security. Do not stay in abusive environments and seek help if you are not secure in your home.

- Cultivate rewarding relationships and distance yourself from unrewarding ones.

Devising Your Comprehensive Living Plan

Now we will create a simple plan to stay well and not fall into a pit of despair. Look at the diagram below. You'll see that there is a straight line that indicates wellness. You might undulate a little bit, occasionally having good days and bad days, but things are generally all right.

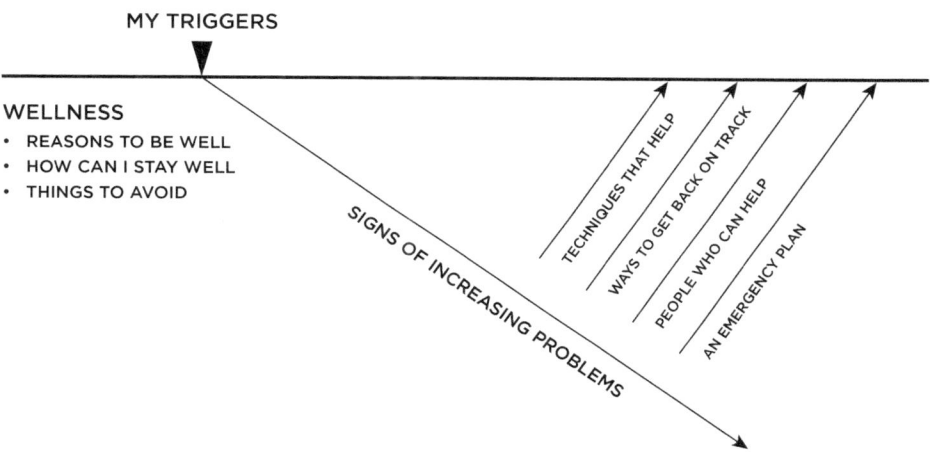

When things start to go wrong, it's usually because something diminishes your capacity to cope. The trigger could be something big, such as losing a job. Or it could be something small, such as doing the dishes when it's not your turn. This tips you over the edge and you're unable to cope.

From here, you might start to slip into despair. At first, there might be signs that you are not coping, such as headaches, sleeplessness or anxiety. If you don't do anything, you could get depressed, have panic attacks or become suicidal. If you continue down this path, you may experience a crisis, a nervous breakdown, a suicide attempt, an overdose or worse.

Example Comprehensive Living Plan

My triggers are:

- Being too stressed at work.
- Drinking too much alcohol.
- Encountering too many rude people.

My warning signs are:

- I get angry or irritable.
- My mind races and I feel anxious.
- I want to quit and move back to my hometown.

These are the healthy things I need to do:

- Take a day off and catch up on sleep.
- Go for a walk, meditate or do some yoga.
- Talk to a friend, hug the cat.

Some things that I've found to be helpful are:

- Reframing my negative thoughts.
- Keeping a regular bedtime schedule.
- Going to counselling or talking to a friend.

This is my emergency plan if I'm ever stuck:

- Call my parents and let them know that I'm feeling depressed.
- Go to my GP or the emergency department if I feel suicidal.
- Stay with a friend if I don't feel safe.

Example 'Staying Okay' Plan

Some reasons why I need to stay well:

- I'm a caring person and my wellbeing is vital for my children and family.
- Getting depressed is difficult and I don't want to feel that way again.
- Looking after my mental health keeps me on track with my work and relationships.

The things I need to do each day to stay well are:

- Have breakfast, take my medications and have a cup of coffee.
- Get out of the house at least once a day.
- Talk to at least one person a day (family or a friend).

These are things I should not do because they mess up my wellness:

- Drink alcohol.
- Blame myself for the past.
- Stop or skip my medications.

I want to share my plan with these people so they can help me stay well:

- Stacy and Carroll.
- Mum and dad.
- My neighbour, Mark.

SIMPLIFY YOUR LIFE

A way to reduce your brain's demands and improve your focus can start with something as simple as having a clean house or office. You can lighten the load by having fewer outgoings. Perhaps you have two cars when you only need one. Maybe someone or something is taking up your time and you could set some boundaries. Look at your list of goals and ask yourself if they are realistic. Perhaps you need to fine-tune them. For example, can you become proficient at Photoshop, learn computer animation, get a PhD, pay off a house and become a gym certified trainer at the same time? Set your priorities and pick a focus. Find ways to simplify your existence and focus on what's important to you and your wellness.

9.
WHAT YOU HAVE LEARNT ABOUT YOURSELF

You should now have some insights into your personality traits and whether you have a mental health problem or trauma that needs to be addressed. You might have negative cognitions, unhelpful feelings or maybe an addiction. Write a brief report on everything we have encountered so far. I'll remind you of the main steps so far.

1. The Four Ls

How will you improve your livelihood?
_____
_____
_____

How will you improve your relationships?
_____
_____
_____

How will you improve your mental health and physical health?
_____
_____
_____

In what ways are you getting into trouble with the law or experiencing other negative consequences?

2. Substances

Now reflect on the data from the Alcohol Basic Screen and Substance Use Basic Screen. Remember, addressing a substance use issue can have a colossal impact on your cognitive function, mood, anxiety, and physical and mental health. I recommend seeking professional help, but that all depends on your readiness to change.

Do you have a substance use problem?

How do you plan to address this issue?

3. Negative Cognitions

Do you have negative cognitions you need to address?

4. Personality Factors – OCEAN

What are your strengths and what do you think needs improvement?

Openness vs Concreteness

Conscientiousness vs Lack of Conscientiousness

Extroversion vs Introversion

Agreeableness vs Disagreeableness

Neuroticism vs Emotional Stability

5. Unhelpful Core Beliefs

Reflect on your unhelpful core beliefs. Perhaps you fear what other people think about you or you're a perfectionist. Write them down.

_____
_____
_____
_____
_____
_____
_____
_____

Hopefully, you were able to write down a few points about the topics we have discussed so far. It is essential to acknowledge this information about yourself to notice and prevent any traps for your current and future self. Don't let this become a beat-up session. You have identified some vulnerabilities, but you have no doubt also recognised many things that are working in your favour.

Use this information to write a summary of what you have learnt about yourself. Now that you have begun to know yourself, this is an essential part of the process. Here's an example:

> I'm a survivor of past trauma and this has made me stronger. I now realise that life is, indeed, a challenge. I know I have to 'upskill' to manage. I'm a person who is quite open to new ideas, and this will be useful because I can try new ways of helping myself. For example, I have focused on resistance training in the past, which was an excellent way to address my fitness. This time I might be more flexible and explore mindfulness and yoga. I have a drinking problem, so I am going to try to work on that. I drink because of negative cognitions. I tend to be hard on myself and I am going to try to work on that too. I've identified some of my unhelpful core beliefs, one of which is seeking the approval of others. I will focus on my happiness instead.

Summarise what you have learnt about yourself.

_____
_____
_____
_____
_____
_____
_____
_____
_____
_____
_____
_____
_____
_____
_____
_____
_____
_____
_____

Readiness to Change

Now that you understand what might be going wrong for you, you need to ask yourself, 'Do I want to change?' If your answer is, 'I can't be bothered', 'I don't think I have a problem', 'I'm happy being a bit miserable because I'm used to it' or 'I have a fear of changing', then you may not have been ready for this guide. Maybe you're not strong enough to make a change yet. That's okay. You always know where to find this training if you need it in the future. There is a saying: 'You can lead a horse to water, but you can't make it drink'.

Whether you drink or not, I respect your decision. Thanks for joining me up to this point. However, if you have any concerns about your wellbeing or mental health and feel that this guide was not helpful, seek advice by calling a helpline, emergency services (if in crisis) or visit your general practitioner.

Getting Organised

How do we take what we've covered so far and make it into a plan? Throughout this guide, you have reflected and made goals. Now you need to list all your planned actions and order them from most important to least important. After doing this, prioritise your list into five or so duties (depending on the task's size and difficulty) to focus on that month. If I was a nursing student, my only job for the month would be to focus on my studies because passing my course is vital to all my other goals. Make sure you review your list regularly so you know what you are doing, what still needs to be done and how you are progressing. Below is an example.

Example Basic Needs Plan

BUILDING INSIGHT - HEALTH BASICS		
The Four Ls (see p. 7)	Alcohol – Basic Screen (see p. 11)	Substance Use – Basic Screen (see p. 12)
Livelihood – Notes: Job is okay. Love – Goal: I need a less negative relationship. Liver – Goal: To improve my fitness and lose 10 kg. To stop eating sugar and processed carbs (corn chips and biscuits). Law – Notes: Never been in trouble.	Notes: Sometimes I drink too much at parties. Goal: Limit myself to six drinks on a night out.	Notes: I'm using marijuana as a crutch to manage my anxiety. Goal: Give up marijuana.
Mental Illness Basic Screen (see p. 13)		Cognition (see p. 16)
Notes: Good – I don't need to see anyone right now. However, my mind races and I get too anxious at night and in the morning. Goal: I want to be more relaxed, resilient and calmer.		Notes: Because I manage a caseload, work problems are always on my mind, even when I'm at home. Goal: I need a job that will allow me to keep my work and private lives separate.

BUILDING INSIGHT – PERSONALITY AND THINKING			
Negative Thinking (see p. 19)	**Core Beliefs** (see p. 36)	**Johari Window** (see p. 52)
Notes: I tend to think negatively and tell myself that I can't do things – whether it be exercise, yoga or meditation. Goal: I need to think calm thoughts. The voice telling me that I can't do it is an 'old echo'. I have exercised before and I can do it again.	Notes: I want to achieve things all the time. Because of this, I am never happy with where I am. I compare myself to others and then I get negative and depressed. Goal: I need to keep trying, but I can't get too attached to the results – as long as I am moving forward. Stay motivated!	Notes: I have decided that an 'outside' perspective could help me deal with my anxious thoughts. Goal: See a counsellor for a few sessions. Goal: A personal trainer may help me understand why I struggle with an exercise regime. Maybe I'll get some good feedback.
Trauma Screening (see p. 57)		**Personality Traits** (see p. 27)
Notes: I have memories of past situations that create negative emotions. But they are not traumas; they're mistakes I've made. Goal: To cope by telling myself 'the feeling will pass' and doing something that will distract me.		Notes: I have a good balance of openness and conscientiousness. Goal: I can be more agreeable by making sure I get enough sleep, eat well (indigestion makes me grumpy) and don't overload myself with jobs. Goal: I can be less neurotic by doing deep breathing, yoga and meditation. Goal: Try not to be introverted 100 per cent of the time. Go out once a week with a friend. I usually enjoy it. Use it or lose it, I guess.

What you have learnt about yourself

STARTING CHANGE – SETTING THE STAGE		
Basic Needs (see p. 39)	**Safety** (see p. 59)	**Relationships** (see p. 59)
Notes: Prioritise sleep, food, shelter and exercise. Notes: Doing okay, but I stay up too late. Goal: Go to bed and wake up at the same time each day.	Notes: I need a non-abusive environment that is physically and psychologically secure, where I am respected and where I can grow, and that doesn't enable my bad habits. Notes: My current partner is psychologically abusive. Goal: Find a more rewarding relationship.	Notes: Cultivate rewarding relationships and distance unrewarding ones. Goal: Start walking with Susan. She's motivated and helps me think more positively.
Personal Growth (see p. 59)		**Fulfilment of Potential** (see p. 59)
Notes: Plan to reduce my victimhood. I want to grow stronger, calmer, saner and wiser. I want to become a good human being. Goal: Work through *Becoming Unshakable*.		Notes: Being what I can be, as much as luck, body and mind allow. Goal: Being better than the old me. Not comparing my progress to other people's.

COMPREHENSIVE LIVING PLAN		
Manage triggers/ Avoid Problems (see pp. 61-63)	**Maintain Supports** (see pp. 61-63)	**Stay Well/Manage Crises/ Stay Safe** (see pp. 61-63)
Goal: Don't answer the phone if dad (trigger) calls. Only see him if mum is there.	Goal: Keep in contact with mum.	Goal: Stay home if I'm not well.

Simplify Your Life (see pp. 64)	Be Ready to Deal with Suffering (see pp. 60)
Goal: Remove all the old crap around the house and garage, like boxes of old clothes, unused books and broken stuff.	Goal: Get my certification as a lifeguard (alternative job option).

STREAMLINE YOUR FOCUS

List of Goals in Order of Importance

Find a less negative relationship.
Remove all the old crap around the house.
Stop bringing work issues home.
Get my certification as a lifeguard (alternative job option).
Start deep breathing, yoga and meditation.
Give up marijuana.
Stop eating sugar and processed carbs (corn chips and biscuits).
Limit myself to six drinks on a night out.
Improve my fitness and lose 10 kg.
See a counsellor for a few sessions.
Stay motivated.
Find a personal trainer.
Improve my ability to cope by telling myself that the feeling will pass.
Become more agreeable by getting enough sleep, eating right and not overloading myself.
Keep in contact with mum.
Don't answer the phone if dad (trigger) calls. Only see him if mum is there.
Being better than the old me. Not comparing my progress to other people's.
Become more relaxed, resilient and calmer.
Think calm thoughts.
Go to bed and wake up at the same time each day.
Work through Becoming Unshakable.
Start walking with Susan. She helps me think more positively.
Try not to be introverted 100 per cent of the time.
Stay home if I'm not well.

What you have learnt about yourself

STREAMLINE YOUR FOCUS		
Month 1 Top Five Goals	**Month 2** Top Five Goals	**Month 3** Top Five Goals
Find a less negative relationship. Remove all the old crap around the house. Find a job that will help me keep my work and private lives separate. Get my certification as a lifeguard (alternative job option). Start deep breathing, yoga and meditation.	Start deep breathing, yoga and meditation. Give up marijuana. Stop eating sugar and processed carbs (corn chips and biscuits). Limit myself to six drinks on a night out. Improve my fitness and lose 10 kg.	Improve my fitness and lose 10 kg. See a counsellor for a few sessions. Stay motivated Find a personal trainer. Improve my ability to cope by telling myself that the feeling will pass.

Complete Your Own Basic Needs Plan

BUILDING INSIGHT - HEALTH BASICS		
The Four Ls (see p. 7)	Alcohol - Basic Screen (see p. 11)	Substance Use - Basic Screen (see p. 12)
Mental Illness Basic Screen (see p. 13)		Cognition (see p. 16)

What you have learnt about yourself

BUILDING INSIGHT – PERSONALITY AND THINKING		
Negative Thinking (see p. 19)	Core Beliefs (see p. 36)	Johari Window (see p. 52)
Trauma Screening (see p. 57)		Personality Traits (see p. 27)

STARTING CHANGE – SETTING THE STAGE		
Basic Needs (see p. 59)	Safety (see p. 59)	Relationships (see p. 59)
Personal Growth (see p. 59)		Fulfilment of Potential (see p. 59)
COMPREHENSIVE LIVING PLAN		
Manage triggers/ Avoid Problems (see pp. 61-63)	Maintain Supports (see pp. 61-63)	Stay Well/Manage Crises/ Stay Safe (see pp. 61-63)

What you have learnt about yourself

Simplify Your Life (see pp. 64)	Be Ready to Deal with Suffering (see pp. 60)

STREAMLINE YOUR FOCUS

List of Goals in Order of Importance

STREAMLINE YOUR FOCUS		
Month 1 Top Five Goals	Month 2 Top Five Goals	Month 3 Top Five Goals

What you have learnt about yourself

CONCLUSION

Congratulations! If you've come this far, you will have discovered many insights about yourself. Whether you have unaccomplished goals or unhelpful core beliefs, you now have the tools to address them.

Remember, achieving any goal requires attention to smaller skills and accomplishments, such as being organised, getting the fundamentals right or mastering emotions or thoughts that limit you. Focus on what needs to happen today, whether it's big or small, and take action. You will experience a more prosperous tomorrow because of this consistent approach. Keep adapting, reflecting and changing – that is the one great rule of life. What's more, seek balance, push yourself forward and be kind to yourself. I wish you a long and joyous life!

The next title in this series will build on the skills you've learnt in this book. It will explore the idea of authenticity and ask critical questions about who you are and what your calling in life might be. If you think this would be of interest to you, join me in the next book!

INDEX

abusive relationship 56
adaptability, as a goal 3
adoration, unhelpful core belief 48
agreeableness 32
alcohol, screening for 11
assumed pattern-finding 19
assuming others' reactions 19
assuming the outcome 19
attainment, as unhelpful core belief 50
authenticity 82
balance 34
basic needs 58
tips 60
plan 71
plan, complete your own 76
blind-self room 53
Buddha 34
Buddhism, as philosophical basis
for this book 3
change - starting/setting the stage for ... 73
change, and motivational interviewing (MI)
as this book's modality 3
change, as a fundamental truth 2
childhood abuse 56
cognitive behavioural therapy (CBT) ... 3, 25
cognitive processes 16
comprehensive living plan 61
example 62, 73
concrete, being 30
conscientiousness 31
control 2
controlling 48
core beliefs 36

crisis 61
dealing with suffering, example 74
dharma 34
disagreeableness 32
discrimination 56
Elementary OCEAN Test 28
emergency plan 62
emotional instability 32
emotional stability 33
enlightenment 34
entropy 2
existentialism, as philosophical basis
for this book 3
extroversion 32
false mea culpa 20
fault-finding, as unhelpful core belief 50
flexibility, as a goal 3
focus 64
Four Ls, tool 7
fulfilment of potential 59
goals 64
gratefulness, as an antidote 2
harmony 34
hidden-self room 54
insight, building of 71
insights, personal 66
intellectual quotient (IQ) 16
introversion 32
Johari window 52
kindness 34
Law, Four Ls tool 8
Livelihood, Four Ls tool 7
Liver, Four Ls tool 8

Index

locus of control	48
Love, Four Ls tool	7
Maslow, Abraham	58
mountain out of a molehill	20
mental illness, basic screen	13
Middle Way, the	34
morality	34
natural disasters	56
needs, hierarchy of	58
negative biasing	19
negative thinking styles	19
neuroticism	33
non-conscientiousness	31
obligation, as unhelpful core belief	51
openness	30
open-self room	53
organising self-improvement	71
personality	27
phenomenology, as philosophical basis for this book	3
physical abuse	56
physiological needs	59
pigeonholing	20
planned actions	71
polarised thinking	19
positive blindfold	20
pragmaticism, as philosophical basis for this book	3
priorities	64
privilege, as unhelpful core belief	51
psychological abuse	56
psychology, and tools in this book	3
as evidence base	3
psychopathy	33
psychosocial circumstances	59
puritan thinking	20
readiness to change	70
realistic cognition	23
rewrite your narrative, as sequel to this book	3
safety needs	59
self-observation	6
signs of not coping	61
simplify your life	64
example	74
social needs	59
stoicism, as philosophical basis for this book	3
streamlining your focus, timing	75
examples	74
suffering, as a fundamental truth	2
summary of self-reflection	69
supports	63
T-10 screening tool	56
trauma	56
treating emotions as facts	20
triggers	61
substance use	12
unhelpful core belief tool	36
unknown-self room	54
validation, unhelpful core belief	48
victimhood, unhelpful core belief	52
warning signs	62
wellness	61
plan to stay well	63
wisdom, as goal	3

ABOUT THE AUTHOR

KARL-HEINZ SCHRADT was born in Germany and moved to New Zealand in his childhood. He graduated with a Health Science degree and immediately specialised in mental health. He has spent more than 20 years counselling people of all ages in forensic, community and acute inpatient settings in New Zealand, the United Kingdom and Australia. He has also completed Postgraduate Diplomas in Health Science and Education, and trained undergraduate Health Science students in clinical practice. Karl-Heinz currently works as an educator in mental health services in Australia.

www.ingramcontent.com/pod-product-compliance
Lightning Source LLC
Chambersburg PA
CBHW060501010526
44118CB00018B/2493